MW01488034

Corinthian Elders

*knowledge makes arrogant
but love edifies*

Jack Fortenberry

Credits

Bridgepointe Publishing Company
1929 Spillway Road, Suite B
Brandon, MS 39047

Published 2008
Revised 2011

Library of Congress Control Number: 2009901013
ISBN 978-0-615-26282-6
ISBN 0-615-26282-1

Dedicated to:

Edi

Thanks to:

Brent, Clark, Jeff, Richard, Sarah & Tedo

Index

Prologue

The inhabits of earth said, *let us make for ourselves a name*, Genesis 11:4, as they purposed and built the Babylonian tower. But Jesus says, *I am the vine, you are the branches; he who abides in Me and I in him, he bears much fruit.*

The purpose of this essay is to encourage a biblical examination of the role of Christian preacher and teacher in order that we may enjoy the one-on-one relationship with our Savior that He designed.

The absence of a New Testament model for the present role of preachers or leaders has not slowed the prevalence of the current model of one or two elders leading a congregation of followers since the time of Constantine. But Scripture warns us of being defrauded of our prize by following leaders in the church. Not just bad leaders but leaders.

By eliminating our use of a favorite teacher and turning to New Testament commands in order to grow in the knowledge of our Father, we will have an unobstructed view of Christ. By our progress in understanding and trusting the person and character of Jesus Christ, God will grow us into conformity with His joy, holiness and loving kindness.

But we all, with unveiled face, beholding as in a mirror the glory of the Lord, are being transformed into the same image from glory to glory, just as from the Lord, the Spirit. II Corinthians 3:18

Seeing that His divine power has granted to us everything pertaining to life and godliness, through the true knowledge of Him who called us by His own glory and excellence. II Peter 1:3

Sometimes in zeal for sanctification and to find favor with God my attention has been on teachings and regimens of prayer or bible readings and even church duties. But II Corinthians 3:18 and II Peter 1:3 tell us that our transformation is being accomplished through the revelation of the character of Christ. The character of our Lord is revealed by the truths of Scripture and also in the application of our knowing and trusting Him. This is where I hope to stay.

I believe the result of this one-on-one relationship of trusting and loving Jesus will then be evident in our joy and fellowship with God's children. *The one who loves his brother abides in the Light and there is no cause for stumbling in him.* I John 2:10.

CORINTHIAN ELDERS

A Painted Picture

It had been days since the missionaries left the makeshift airstrip and climbed through the jungle following the river upstream. Spirits on the team were controlled and resolute. Who could have foreseen the unfolding of history during the last twenty years? From closed communist communities in China and Cuba had come such a witness from God working within the hearts of believers that the entire world had taken notice.

First it was only a blip on the screen as Christian charity from these developing countries began to overshadow humanitarian aid from huge industrial economies as the United States. While denominations analyzed the phenomenon for clues, the surge continued from the change in the lives of those communist believers. The character of churches began to change all over the world.

Church goers, hungry for the Spirit and with hearts set on the Kingdom, had left their favorite pew in order to 'be the church' and not 'go to church.' Less and less were heard the words, 'good sermon', and more and more was the love of the brethren observed in local assemblies. Evangelism was occurring across backyard fences instead of from pulpits. Dots of small assemblies permeated neighborhoods, countries and continents in numbers amazing even to the believers themselves.

Where once denominational differences had absorbed time and expense, many differences simply did not arise as brothers in Christ focused on who Christ was, what He had done and what He was doing. Other differences were discussed circumspectly with open Bibles on kitchen and patio tables.

As pastors had reconsidered Scriptural teaching on the role of elders many moved to church planting missions. This caused evangelism with unreached people groups to explode. Some pastors had sought to serve politically or as teachers and the social landscape of every country had been affected.

Funds previously spent on maintenance of church buildings and church staffs were flooding into mission agencies and hospitals. When in past ages greed and selfish motives had been ascribed to the church, now giving and serving was seen so purely selfless not even detractors of the gospel could whisper against her.

Not that sin in the world had ceased; just the opposite. But the contrast caused the light of the gospel to shine even brighter. The influx of faithful men and resources had charged like an army into the darkness of all societies but especially unreached people groups who had never before, except from shadowy tribal legends, heard the special revelation that God had come to earth as a man, fellowshipped with us, suffered and died for our sins. From conversions of tribesmen had arisen tribal elders, deacons and evangelists who in turn knew of souls dispersed throughout the mountain jungles and previously unknown tribes were found for advancement of the Kingdom.

Was it possible we were closing in on all unreached people groups with the gospel?

Our mission team had departed from civilization knowing the martyrs that previously attempted to reach these souls. There was absolutely no evidence the outcome would be any different this time, but the team continued knowing in their heart the joy and peace of serving a loving Father.

The encounter with the tribe was sudden and completely unexpected. Hearts pounded as the interpreter explained the reason for the intrusion. Throughout the night discussions were held around outdoor fires; while around the globe prayers were offered. Then an all powerful God took pleasure in the salvation of His children.

Missionaries and tribesmen alike thought dawn was breaking on the mountain when they turned as one gasping at the beauty. Then they joined the rest of mankind in bowing every knee.

Leading is Misleading

My optimism in the painted picture comes from a belief that God is continuing to work in His church by moving us toward a more biblical role for elders. As the body of Christ trusts Him by following New Testament examples, the bright beam of the Gospel will intensify.

Jesus told us in John 15:3-5:

Abide in Me, and I in you. As the branch cannot bear fruit of itself unless it abides in the vine, so neither can you unless you abide in Me. I am the vine, you are the branches; he who abides in Me and I in him, he bears much fruit, for apart from Me you can do nothing.

These verses tell us that only by abiding in Christ may we glorify and enjoy Him. We admire and thank those from whom we have heard God's Word both for salvation and edification, but is it possible our attention may actually be diverted from Christ when we look to gifted Christian preachers and teachers? Was this not the situation in I Corinthians 1-4? Consider Paul's instruction to the Corinthians that their *...faith would not rest on the wisdom of men but on the power of God.* I Corinthians 2:5.

Corinth

For if you were to have countless tutors in Christ... I
Corinthians 4:15.

As *wise* men debated their interpretations of
apostolic teaching they drew followings of
Corinthian believers who *zealously* desired *solid
food.* At least some were drawn believing they
were correctly following Pauline or Petrine
theology. These members of the body compared
words of Paul, Peter and Apollos.

Divisions appeared among the believers who were
attracted to various teachings of men. These were
doctrinally solid men being followed! An almost
imperceptible diversion from their relationship
with Christ to men caused jealousy and strife
instead of encouragement to love one another in
that assembly.

*...Since there is jealousy and strife among you, are you
not fleshly, and are you not walking like mere men? For
when one says, 'I am of Paul,' and another, 'I am of
Apollos,' are you not mere men?* I Corinthians 3:3-4.

Paul responded by reminding those believers they
possessed the very Spirit of God. In I Corinthians
3:16 Paul says, *Do you not know that you are a temple
of God and that the Spirit of God dwells in you?* In
3:21-23 he explains, *So then let no one boast in men.
For all things belong to you, whether Paul or Apollos or
Cephas or the world or life or death or things present or*

things to come; all things belong to you, and you belong to Christ; and Christ belongs to God.

Notice Paul was not rebuking their lack of loving each other, although that is implicit. The rebuke was the assembly's focus on teachers, *So then let no one boast in men.* Paul reminded the Corinthians of their personal relationship with God through his Word. When the Corinthians turned their eyes from Christ to men the branches were girded and the connection to the vine impaired. Jealousy and strife ensued.

To discourage the Corinthians from focusing on men, Paul instructed them to teach themselves, *...when you assemble, each one has a psalm, has a teaching, has a revelation, has a tongue, has an interpretation...for edification...* I Corinthians 14:26.

For the church to present one or a few preachers to a passive audience who attend services because they enjoy the sermons or preaching style is a violation of Paul's commandment to the Corinthians when he redirected them from men to Christ. Why do we persist in disregarding this commandment? Do we know better than Paul?

<u>Colossae</u>

Another example of Paul's concern for believers turning from their Head to leaders of the church is in the Book of Colossians. In the context of ecclesiastical 'authorities' in Colossians 1:18; 2:8,

10, 15, 19 and 20, Paul expresses his apprehension for the two house churches at Colossae and Laodicea, *For I want you to know how great a struggle I have on your behalf and for those who are at Laodicea.* Colossians 2:1.

See to it that no one takes you captive through philosophy and empty deception, according to the <u>tradition</u> (teaching) *of men, according to the* <u>elementary principles</u> (rules) *of the world, rather than according to Christ.* Colossians 2:8. Whether the Colossians were holding to teachers or men in authority, Paul was disturbed that they were disconnected from their Head, Colossians 2:19.

In Colossians 2:18 he said, *Let no one keep defrauding you of your prize* and he pointed the Colossians back to Christ in 3:1, *if you have been raised up with Christ, keep seeking the things above, where Christ is seated at the right hand of God.*

To redirect the believers from looking to men and facilitate them in *seeking the things above* in 3:16 Paul again commanded, *Let the Word of Christ richly dwell within you, with all wisdom teaching and admonishing one another.*

The point once again was if the Colossians had the Spirit of God dwelling in them why were they looking to men's teachings or authorities? They had God's law written in their hearts.

Two churches, same problem, same solution.

God's revelation through His Word

...after those days, says the LORD: I will put My laws into their minds, and I will write them on their hearts. And I will be their God, and they shall be My people. And they shall not teach everyone his fellow citizen, and everyone his brother, saying, 'Know the LORD', for all will know me, from the least to the greatest... Hebrews 8:10-11.

Believers in Corinth and Colossae shared a desire to pursue Christ but they lost their connection to the vine by not trusting His love and indwelling. They looked from Christ for their solid food to spiritual leaders.

In John 16:13-14 Christ gave us this promise, *...when He, the Spirit of truth, comes, He will guide you into all the truth; .....He will glorify Me, for He will take of Mine and will disclose it to you.* Try reading this passage with emphasis on the word 'will' to understand the certainty of that truth.

This promise of God to personally teach his children is yet more proof of his amazing grace. How glorious is this thought that each of us, if regenerate, can know the joy of His personal teaching from His Word. How worldly we are if after experiencing the revelation of His character and the veracity of His Word we rely on men to lead us into spiritual truth.

Now we have received, not the spirit of the world, but the Spirit who is from God, so that we may know the things freely given to us by God…not in words taught by human wisdom. I Corinthians 2:12-13.

But doesn't the Spirit work <u>through</u> gifted men, *eloquent and mighty,* like Apollos, Acts 18:24? Certainly! But back to the danger of which Paul warned us. Our duty is, yes, to learn from them, while testing their teaching with a Berean spirit, but 'job one' is to keep our eyes on our Savior and His personal teaching through His Word. Perhaps a barometer of how well we are doing is to examine ourselves. Would our relationship with other believers be described as in unity? If not, perhaps disunity, or even apathy, is evidence our eyes are not on Christ alone for salvation and edification. *The one who loves his brother abides in the Light* (Christ) *and there is no cause for stumbling in him.* I John 2:10.

Does a noticeable shift in membership when a gifted preacher moves to another church reflect relationships that are more man-centered than Christ-centered? Where was the love among those members previously assembled who had shared the Lord's Table? Was this division like the historical events in Corinth? Using I John 2:10 as a barometer to ascertain the congregation's relationship with Christ those church members did not have a close relationship to Him even though they felt very close to their departed leader. Even an imperceptible reliance on the strength or knowledge of leaders as occurred in Corinth may harm our relationship with Jesus.

Paul would have pointed that congregation back to Christ: *So then let no one boast in men. For all things belong to you, whether Paul or Apollos or Cephas or the world or life or death or things present or things to come; all things belong to you, and you belong to Christ; and Christ belongs to God.* I Corinthians 3:21-23.

To Preach or Not to Preach

So what is the point of this essay? Well, the point is simply that we are guilty of not loving each other as were those brothers in Corinth which indicates we are not looking to Christ. Because our joy will only be fulfilled in Him, John 15:11, it would be helpful for us to look <u>less</u> to *eloquent* and *mighty* teachers, as Apollos is described in Acts 18:24, for our understanding and knowledge of Jesus and more to God's Word. In this manner, our relationship with God would be enhanced by His Spirit and demonstrated by a new found love for one another.

Think of yourself as being in an ocean but not quite able to swim. Jesus is there within your reach but also Peter, Paul and Apollos. As Peter, Paul and Apollos describe to you how and why you should reach out to Jesus, you look to one of them and reach to him. In doing so, by necessity, you turn away from Jesus. You know what happens when you do that.

The Apostle John warned that jealousy and strife, as in I Corinthians 1-4, are symptomatic of not walking with Christ. *...If we walk in the Light as He Himself is in the Light, we have fellowship with one another.* I John 1:7.

If we, as believers, did have the same need as those brethren in Corinth or Colossae, then we might reevaluate our use of the pulpit. We would learn everything we could of Christ's person and endeavor to interact with Him. While prayerfully studying our Bibles and remembering He is with us always, we would renew our efforts to love one another starting with our family and those with whom we assemble each week.

As elders we might place less emphasis on our own teaching or gift and put more emphasis on the nurture and development of the flock. Recognizing the Holy Spirit within each believer, we should point them again and again toward Christ until they are filled with confidence of God's presence within them.

Since looking <u>less</u> to pastors or elders might be considered a sin by many, let's read what the Bible says about the elder's function. Applying the elder's role that is prescribed in the Bible will enable us to please God and better serve the kingdom. We need to read what the Bible says because in today's organized church the elder's role is not always the same as outlined in the New Testament nor the traditional role before Constantine.

For instance, should we have one or two elders who we charge with preaching because of their call or gift? How else should we do this? Did not God ordain by 'called' men preaching the word that His Kingdom would be advanced? *How then will they call on Him in whom they have not believed? How will they believe in Him whom they have not heard? And how will they hear without a preacher?* Romans 10:14. And with such a 'calling' should not gifted and trained men in our assemblies teach our lesser trained or 'un-called' men?

Well, certainly God did call believers to proclaim the gospel and teach, but let us not fulfill our duty by hiring out this obligation to professional preachers. Acts 8:4 indicates all of us should be 'preaching' not just a few gifted teachers, *Therefore, those who had been scattered went about preaching the word.*

Giftedness, as some consider oratory skills in professional preachers, may in fact be detrimental to a demonstration of the Spirit's working as indicated by Paul in I Corinthians 2:4, *my message and my preaching were not in persuasive words of wisdom.* This is not to say God does not expect us to be industrious in our study and use of Scripture. Certainly that is not the case as in II Timothy 2:15.

The church meeting prescribed by Paul was very different from what many believers experience in churches across the United States. Whereas contemporary church services are usually led by one or two professionally trained pastors or elders with a scripted program of hymns, prayers and a sermon, I Corinthians 14:26-31 describes interactive meetings of believers with no professional speaker, no script and many sermons by both new and old believers. Everyone was encouraged to participate without emphasizing any gifts over others.

Perhaps this interactive participation by everyone was especially commanded in Corinth because of their intellectual interest in teaching. But Corinth was not an isolated case because the Ephesians were given the same instructions for everyone to participate, Ephesians 5:19, as well as the Colossians, Colossians 3:16.

In I Timothy 5:17, elders who worked hard at preaching and teaching were honored but in context of the church assembly, no individual's teaching was emphasized more than others nor was the teaching gift more important than other gifts. In I Corinthians 14:26 Paul commanded, *....when you assemble, each one has a psalm, has a teaching, has a revelation, has a tongue, has an interpretation. Let all things be done for edification.*

This does not violate James' command in James 3:1 when he says, *Let not many of you become teachers, my brethren, knowing that as such we will incur a stricter judgment.* Scripture does not contradict itself. James 3:1 simply elaborates on I Corinthians 14:26. Teaching is integral, but participating by bringing a psalm, a hymn, a praise, a revelation of what our Father has taught us is wonderful and commanded.

When we assemble, some may need to be encouraged by Paul to participate, whereas, others may need encouragement from James to be more disciplined and refrain from teaching as often or too long. It may not be edifying for the <u>entire</u> body to spend time on protracted lessons during our assembly together. Whatever the reason, this is the commandment from Scripture if for no other purpose than to not focus on teachers as at Corinth.

But didn't Paul preach until midnight in Acts 20:7? Some versions did use the English word 'preach' but the Greek word #1256, *dialegomai*, indicates this was a two-way dialogue. Paul interacted and talked with those at Troas.

That interactive meeting at Troas could serve as an example for us today. If a meeting of believers becomes too large for orderly interaction and shepherding, then a church split should be considered and not a larger temple. These church splits should be encouraging and not the result of jealousy or strife.

Why did we change how the church met? One possibility is that assemblies chose gifted speakers to eliminate divisions that occurred in interactive meetings. This could have been similar to the adoption of confessions by churches in order to avoid disputes. Maybe other groups preferred 'good preaching' to interaction between believers and thus succumbed to 'tickling of ears' in spite of the warning by Paul in II Timothy 4:3. But from all evidence the biblical pattern was dropped when Constantine moved assemblies of believers into huge temples of pagan deities and the pure size of these mega churches precluded interactive meetings.

An objection might be that many church members are not trained. Don't we need seminary trained men in order to teach accurately?

Certainly seminary training is a blessing. The original Hebrew and Greek which believers learn is great and the theology may be helpful, but nothing satisfies the child of God like God's Word. By God's Word I mean Scripture. Ecclesiology, church history, homiletics, and contrived applications may tickle our ears but they will not satisfy the thirsty child of God. Jesus says: *My sheep hear My voice, and I know them, and they follow Me* in John 10:27. My experience with interactive meetings is that more Scripture is covered than with expository sermons. We simply have to trust Paul in this regard. He told the Colossians in 3:16 all should participate in these meetings.

By training or giftedness some brothers may bless us, as Apollos blessed Corinth, with their handling of Scripture, illustrations or theology. But if we ask other brethren to be quiet so we might listen to Apollos all morning, what an imbalance that is. To correct this imbalance at Corinth, Paul reminded them, *Love never fails; But if there are gifts of prophecy, they will be done away; if there are tongues, they will cease; if there is knowledge, it will be done away.* I Corinthians 13:8.

The assembling of saints in the New Testament was not about sermons as much as it was enjoying the Lord's Supper together (Acts 20:7, I Corinthians 11:20) seeing God in their midst and encouraging one another in the faith. We see God in the lives of other believers. We see God when believers express their love for us and others. Listening to a sermon or lecture may be helpful, interesting and even entertaining, but Paul did not want the assembly of saints focused on a sermon or a teacher.

Should not the church be a growing, evolving entity as we grow wiser and are faced with new situations? For instance, is not the church more efficient with one or two preachers and a set order of service? No. Paul was very specific when he commanded, ...*stand firm and hold to the traditions which you were taught, whether by word of mouth or by letter from us.* II Thessalonians 2:15.

In I Corinthians 11:16 he was emphatic when some wanted to change the pattern of the church, *If one is inclined to be contentious, we have no other practice, nor have the churches of God.* Paul gave the church clear instructions and examples of how to function and he chastised the believers when they did not follow his teaching. Paul did this because he wanted them to hold to Christ.

Teaching One Another

'Let not the vain speeches of any trouble you and draw you aside from the truth...'

From verse 4, of the purported Epistle of Paul the Apostle to the Laodiceans, Quaker Translation based on Sixtus Senensis MSS in Sorbonne Library, Paris and the Library of Joannes a Viridario, Padua and also the British Museum under Harleian MSS. Cod. 1212 as described on page 94 of The Lost Books of the Bible, published 1979, Testament Books, a division of Random House, Inc., New York.

Well if the preacher doesn't preach, who will?

Some texts limit the number of teachers in an assembly or church meeting. James 3:1 commands that not many of us become teachers. Also, I Corinthians 12:29 asks, *All are not teachers are they?* But in order to understand God's instruction we should look at all Scripture dealing with teaching; and, Scripture also commands that we teach one another.

Let the Word of Christ richly dwell within you, with all wisdom teaching and admonishing one another... Colossians 3:16.

...by this time you ought to be teachers... Hebrews 5:12.

...if all prophesy, and an unbeliever or an ungifted man enters, he is convicted by all... I Corinthians 14:24.

...when you assemble, each one has a psalm, has a teaching, has a revelation, has a tongue, has an interpretation...for edification... I Corinthians 14:26.

...you can all prophesy one by one, so that all may learn and all may be exhorted... I Corinthians 14:31.

Most of these verses, though applicable anywhere, are in the context of church meetings.

Also, remember these verses commanding us to teach one another are written to the church and not just elders. In fact, elders are rarely directly addressed in most epistles which emphasizes the one-on-one relationship we have with our creator. In the case of the Colossians in 4:16, Paul said, *when this letter is read among you, have it also read in the church of the Laodiceans....*

We rejoice like Paul in I Corinthians 1:4-7 when the body is gifted with teachers. But when this happens we are not to abdicate our duties to participate in teaching one another because God gifted a few. In fact, God enjoys working through our weaknesses. II Corinthians 12:9, 10, Judges 7:2.

If we say we are not able to teach one another we deny God's Spirit in us. *As for you, the anointing which you received from Him abides in you, and you have no need for anyone to teach you; but as His anointing teaches you about all things, and is true and is not a lie, and just as it has taught you, you abide in Him.* I John 2:27.

Paul's requirement that all participate does not mean all should teach by expositing Scriptures. In the assembly we teach each other by singing, by talking about Christ's faithfulness and giving testimony to what God is doing in our lives. We may contribute to the church meeting by reading Scripture, praying or encouraging. Paul gave teaching a lower priority than reading of Scripture or exhortation in I Timothy 4:13, *...give attention to the public reading of Scripture, to exhortation and teaching.*

We all learn in different ways and God's spirit works in different ways. *Now there are varieties of gifts, but the same Spirit. And there are varieties of ministries, and the same Lord. There are varieties of effects, but the same God who works all things in all persons. But to each one is given the manifestation of the Spirit for the common good.* I Corinthians 12:4-7. Again, the context of this text is in the assembly or church meeting of the Corinthians.

When Paul heard the Corinthians were following teachers to the neglect of other gifts he said in I Corinthians 4:20: *For the Kingdom of God does not consist in words but in power.* Of course we are fed by God's Word but Paul was making the point that Corinthian teachers were incorrect in their prominent role and he instructed everyone to participate.

The practice of one teacher addressing passive listeners was characteristic of Hellenistic Jews who adopted teaching methods from Greek philosophers. Previously in synagogues Judaizers took turns reading and discussing as Jesus did when he read from Isaiah in Luke 4:16-21. Each believer, including elders, participated in those meetings of the early church. Perhaps it is from a guilty conscience or maybe insecurity about being a *workman who does not need to be ashamed, accurately handling the word of truth* II Timothy 2:15, that drives us to rely so heavily on professional religious teachers, but this is not the relationship Christ desires for us.

Teachers are integral in New Testament discipleship, but a danger exists when we begin to choose favorite teachers and preachers from the body while limiting our interaction with others, James 2:1. This focus may lower our zeal for personal interaction with God's Spirit as we seek His character and pleasure while studying Scripture. Focusing on men's teaching as a substitute for cultivating a relationship with the Holy Spirit may make us languid in our duty to grow in knowledge of Him even though we may be learning about Him.

This favoritism in the assembly may reveal a lack of interest in the brother seated in the pew behind us. It may indicate that we do not desire interaction or information of how Christ is working in his life. When looking to our favorite teachers as our service to God we may minimize the presence of God indwelling other believers whom we consider immature in faith or to whom God has given a different path in life. Conversely, the elimination of favorite teachers will allow us to love one another as we interact and recognize our Father's Spirit in each other.

As elders we should be aware of the danger Paul identified in I Corinthians 1-4. We should ensure our teaching contributions are not protracted or do not encroach on participation by others. Our role should include facilitating participation and encouraging those who are timid.

For decades our society has enjoyed the marvels of sitting passively and enjoying the technology of television. But as internet and broadband became available volumes have been written about the advantage of internet over television for one reason: it is interactive. Is this not what Paul told the Corinthians? Do not passively focus on a few teachers but interact. *When you assemble, each one has a psalm, has a teaching, has a revelation, has a tongue, has an interpretation...for edification...* I Corinthians 14:26.

But, with untrained elders or laity teaching churches, will the flock be exposed to heresies which will confuse the believer or lead them astray?

There is already heresy in the visible church today. Believers are being misled because they are depending on men to lead them in His Word instead of the Holy Spirit. In II Timothy 4:3 Paul writes, *The time will come when they will not endure sound doctrine; but wanting to have their ears tickled, they will accumulate for themselves teachers in accordance to their own desires.* When we think of unsound doctrine many things come to mind but what could be more basic than turning from our 'one another' duties of loving each other to our favorite leaders as did the Corinthians?

Heresies will exist. At least in Paul's model for the church we will have many participating in order to offset or challenge any teaching that is taking away or adding to Scripture. We cannot change hearts but we can follow the traditions Paul installed in churches and heed his warnings not to follow men but Christ. The elder who is not seminary trained may not utilize systematic theologies to teach the flock. I do not apologize for being too simplistic when reminding us, *All Scripture is inspired by God and profitable for teaching, for reproof, for correction, for training in righteousness so that the man of God may be adequate, equipped for every good work.* II Timothy 3:16-17. If the man of God is equipped by Scripture for every good work, exactly what is the additional benefit of those initials behind the name of Reverend such and such?

Jesus, our self-proclaimed jealous God, emphasized He was the only teacher we should recognize. In Matthew 23:8 He says, *Do not be called Rabbi; for One is your Teacher and you are all brothers.* This does not mean we should not teach one another. That would contradict other Scripture given by Christ's Spirit. But it does mean that while learning from one another we should not lean toward an Apollos for understanding because doing so would draw our eyes off our Savior. Notice this verse puts the duty on the teacher to encourage the listener to not rely on the teacher, but instead communicate Jesus is the vine and we are the branches.

By following Paul's model we will continue to be blessed with godly, gifted men but we will also see God at work in every believer. This is important because from the backdrop of ordinary men and women God may be more clearly seen by more people than from the backdrop of a clergy robe.

II Timothy 2:2 states, *the things which you have heard from me in the presence of many witnesses, entrust these to faithful men who will be able to teach others also.* Sometimes we use this verse to hand pick young candidates for seminary but when Paul said, *faithful men who will be able,* he is simply saying men who believe will be able by the empowerment of God's Spirit to teach others. Emphasize the promise as you read that verse. Remember what

Jesus said in John 16:13, *But when He, the Spirit of Truth, comes, He will guide you into all the truth.*

The Holy Spirit will guide converts into all truth. Not that their grammar will improve or their communication skills will change overnight; but God's Spirit will give them a heart to serve and the truth of Christ to share. How to teach one another and accurately handle the word is very important but our relationship with Christ, the vine, is even more important. We will make mistakes, it is not as if professional preachers do not, and guess what? God will perfect those mistakes in us and in those listening. Christ will be faithful if we hold to Him. He promised us.

Ecclesiastical Office

I believe I Corinthians and Colossians are teaching that leaders are misleading. Not because they are not godly men but because the teaching that Paul prescribed had more facets than is usually encompassed in an organized worship service. I certainly want to give honor to hard working elders, especially those who are diligent to teach and preach, but I also want to remember that Christ told us not to have leaders! *Do not be called leaders; for One is your leader, that is Christ.* Matthew 23:10.

So, is the office of elder a governing position?

That is what the Colossian Church thought. The Presbyterian Book of Church Order or a local church as at Colossae may give elders certain governmental authority. But let's consider whether the New Testament gives elders governing authority by examining the Greek passages which discuss a religious 'office' in regards to elders.

Oh, there are none.

Eldership is not an office in the sense of a governing authority in the Greek New Testament.

The English word translated 'office' is from the Greek word *episkope* #1984 which has the general meaning of overseeing or visitation. It occurs one time in the New Testament as the office of an apostle in Acts 1:20. Apostles had authority. They gave us the very words of Scripture which were canonized. *Episkope* in the context of elders is simply not in the New Testament.

Some translations of the New Testament called elder or overseer an office in one verse, I Timothy 3:1. But in <u>Interlinear NIV Parallel New Testament</u> the transliteration says, *If anyone aspires to oversight a good work he desires.* That is all. No 'office.' In <u>Greek to English Interlinear of the New King James Version New Testament</u> it states, *if any stretches forward to overseership a good work he is desirous.* Again, no office.

To recap, though the New Testament refers to Roman offices and Levitical offices it does not refer to an <u>office</u> of elder in the Greek manuscripts.

Are there Greek texts which mention the authority of elders? No.

We are not speaking of apostles. Christ was an apostle, Hebrews 3:1. Apostles had authority as well as an office, Acts 1:20. They could raise the dead and were charged to proclaim the gospel directly by Christ. We are not discussing a believer's authority over sin or spirits, or authority of parents in their family. We are speaking of New Testament elders and whether God ordained elders to have governmental authority over His children in the local church.

A few English versions of the New Testament mention elder authority one time in Hebrews 13:17 *Obey your leaders and submit* to their authority. The English translation to 'their authority' is in neither interlinear Greek text. Look it up. If 'to their authority' was in the Greek text then Hebrews 13:17 would contradict Luke 22:25-26 where Jesus says, *The Kings of the Gentiles lord it over them; and those who have authority over them are called 'Benefactors.' But it is not this way with you, but the one who is the greatest among you must become like the youngest, and the leader like the servant.*

Wait, why should we <u>obey</u> elders if they have no authority?

The word for 'obey' as to a military command as *children be obedient to your parents* in Colossians 3:20, in the Greek New Testament is *hupakouo*, Greek word #5219. The word translated 'obey' in Hebrews 13:17 is *peitho*, Greek word #3982 with the general meaning of trust, be persuaded by or yield to. This is not the same as to obey an authority. There is no other instance in the New Testament that asserts we should obey elders.

We should submit to or be subject to elders, but that is quite different than an elder wielding authority. We are taught to yield to or be persuaded by them, but not as to a military command.

In I Peter 5:5 Peter says, *younger men, likewise, be subject to your elders.* This is important because by contrasting 'elder' with 'younger' elder is not an office but rather a season of the believer's life. This is not necessarily a season of physical age, I Timothy 4:12, but a season in his spiritual life.

Even though we should be subject to elders we do not have a ruling class or caste in the church. This can be seen because we are all commanded to yield to each other, *be subject to one another in the fear of Christ,* in Ephesians 5:21 which completes the cycle of submission in the church. Certainly we should exercise discipline for sin. But we should not discipline someone for disobeying the pastor on an issue concerning a financial budget or a family decision.

Are these words 'office', 'obey' and 'authority' really important? Absolutely. These words are only used one time in translations of the New Testament and not at all in the Greek, as illustrated above, in regards to elders and thus can have the effect of expanding or changing our view of Paul's teaching on the function of elders.

Not only is a system of authority over believers not taught in the New Testament, it is even warned against in Colossians. Paul was talking about submitting to religious authorities when he said,

Let *no one* keep defrauding you of your prize...and not holding fast to the head (Christ)... Colossians 2:18-19.

The focus on men's teaching took the Corinthians' eyes off Christ and it also took the Colossians' eyes off of Him. But Paul was addressing something else at Colossae. He was concerned about governing authorities in the church.

In Colossians 2:8 Paul writes, *See to it that no one takes you captive through philosophy and empty deception, according to the tradition* (teaching) *of men, according to the elementary principles of the world, rather than according to Christ.*

The Greek word #4747 *stoicheion* is interpreted 'elementary principle' and has the general meaning of 'rule.' Read how this word is used in Galatians 4:2-3.

...But he is under guardians and managers until the date set by the father. So also we, while we were children were held in bondage under the 'elemental things' of the world.

Note the repetition of Paul's attention on ruling authorities in the following Colossian verses:

1:16 *...whether thrones or dominions or rulers or authorities...*
1: 18 *...He is also head of the body, the church...*
2:8 *...See to it that no one takes you captive...according to the elementary principles...* (rules)

2:10 ...*He is the head over all rule and authority*...

2:15 ...*When He* (Christ) *had disarmed the rulers and authorities*...

2:16 ...*no one is to act as your judge*...

2:18 ...*let no one give judgment against*... in the Greek from <u>Interlinear NIV Parallel New Testament</u>

2:19 ...*not holding fast to the head*... (of the church, Christ)

2:20 ...*if you have died with Christ to the elementary principles*... (rules)

2:20 ...*why*... *do you submit*...

2:22 ...*commandments and teachings of men*...

Paul identifies ecclesiastical authorities in Colossians 2:16, *Therefore <u>no one is to act as your judge</u> in regard to food or drink or in respect to a festival or a new moon or a Sabbath day.*

Do you see from verse 2:16 that Paul is not as concerned about the Sabbath day as much as he is concerned the believer will submit to an authority as a substitute for Christ's direct lordship? Paul had already told us in Romans 14:5, *One person regards one day above another, another regards every day alike. Each person must be fully convinced in his own mind.* Paul's commandment in verse 16 is *no one is to act as your judge* and not whether they should observe a Sabbath day.

Again in Colossians 2:18, *Let <u>no one</u> keep defrauding you of your prize by delighting in self-abasement* (humility) *and the worship of the angels, taking <u>his</u>*

stand on visions he has seen, inflated without cause by his fleshly mind. Yes, these delights in humility and the worship, or religion, of angels are a problem. Yes, they are actually prideful and redirect the believer's attention from God as well. But Paul's primary concern was the Colossians were *not holding fast to the Head,* Colossians 2:19, because they were submitting to authorities, Colossians 2:20.

Very definitely our fellowship with one another is related to our relationship with Christ, *...if we walk in the Light* (Christ),*...we have fellowship with one another...* I John 1:7. But by submitting to leaders as a substitute for our fellowship with one another, we will loosen our hold on Christ. We must not trade our relationship with Him for a religious system.

Consensus Governance

If the elders are not in charge, who is?

Notice how some passages indicate our Father is as concerned with our corporate condition as He is with our personal condition.

By this all men will know that you are My disciples, if you have love for one another. John 13:35.

Make my joy complete by being of the same mind, maintaining the same love, united in spirit, intent on one purpose. Philippians 2:2.

Now I exhort you, brethren, by the name of our Lord Jesus Christ, that you all agree and that there be no divisions among you, but that you be made complete in the same mind and in the same judgment. I Corinthians 1:10.

Since the New Testament elder did not seem to be a ruler in the sense of a governing authority, let's fit together passages dealing with elders and see how this unity, described above, is supposed to work when we assemble as required by Hebrews 10:25.

Peter exhorts elders in I Peter 5:2-3, *shepherd the flock of God among you, exercising oversight not under compulsion, but voluntarily, according to the will of God; and not for sordid gain, but with eagerness; nor yet as lording it over those allotted to your charge, but proving to be examples to the flock.* Notice when Peter says *flock of God among you* he does not say 'under you.' Also from this verse we are taught the elder is not a governing authority because he is not 'lording' over other believers.

The governing comes from the assembly as a whole. In Matthew 18:17, *If he refuses to listen to them, tell it to the church; and if he refuses to listen even to the church, let him be as a gentile and a tax collector,* Christ instructs the church or assembly to have the final say. Of course this could be a reference to the church which is presupposing elders are making decisions, but since elders are not given this authority anywhere else in the New Testament don't assume that is His intent. Continuing in Matthew 18:19-20, Jesus says, *Again I say to you, that if two of you agree on earth about anything that they may ask, it shall be done for them by My Father who is in heaven. For where two or three have gathered together in My name, I am there in their midst.* This verse is in context of church governance. And it is teaching about consensus.

Although government is by consensus we also need to consider that in several passages elders are charged to protect the flock. Just as King David protected the flock from lions and bears in addition to leading them to food and water, Timothy was instructed to watch for different doctrine, controversial questions, disputes with words, friction and opportunistic men looking for gain, I

Timothy 6:3-5. Unity of the body does not come at any cost and elders were involved in making decisions as to what was and what was not edifying for the body. Likewise, if only one or two members of the body obstruct consensus in a biblical requirement, then elders are needed for shepherding. But, these are opportunities for growth of the whole body. This is not a time to take pride in our spiritual understanding and leave loved ones behind.

Consider what Greek word *proistemi* #4291b teaches us about the duties of elders. It is translated as rule only one time in the New Testament. Hmm. This occurs in I Timothy 5:17. One definition is to preside, govern or superintend per <u>New Analytical Greek Lexicon</u>.

If we use this word definition then elders are placed in a position of presiding over meetings and the flock. So as not to contradict other passages the elders must preside, not with the authority of a puritan preacher preaching to a dutiful congregation or checking on family catechisms, nor as *busybodies*, II Thessalonians 3:11, but by focusing the assembly on Christ, their relationship with Him, and his commandment to love one another.

Another definition of *proistemi* is to undertake resolutely or practice diligently. Using this definition we see elders as our examples giving us encouragement and a model to follow. This definition is supported by *proistemi* #4291b's cousin, *proimos* #4291a. *Proimos* is defined simply as 'early' which brings a chronological aspect into the definition. This would indicate that elders are older in the faith. Surprise.

Titus 3:9-10 is an example of the duty of an elder. *...Avoid foolish controversies and genealogies and strife and disputes about the law, for they are unprofitable and worthless. Reject a factious man after a first and second warning.* We should endeavor to make their job easier by submitting and loving them while weighing their declarations with Scripture as they encourage the assembly toward Christ and unity.

The elders have other duties during the assembly but not in the forefront as much as encouraging the flock to participate and keeping the group on edifying subject matter. Not as Diotrephes, desiring to be first but in the background caring, nurturing, protecting and encouraging the flock, III John 9. The elders described in the New Testament are examples to the flock that are not perfect, I Timothy 5:20, but even in imperfection are a witness of God's indwelling spirit by humbly seeking forgiveness and resolution.

A Diotrephes is great to have if our model is to go to church, sit back in a pew and enjoy a good sermon. But if our consensus model is that we are the church, Diotrephes could discourage younger or quieter souls to participate in the manner Paul prescribed. He might encourage weaker brothers or sisters to look to him instead of seeking Christ's personal teaching through His Word.

These texts portray elders who are as submissive to the assembly as those assembled are willing to yield to their guidance, *Those* (elders) *who continue in sin, rebuke in the presence of all, so that the rest also will be fearful of sinning.* I Timothy 5:20. The elders are allowing the flock to grow and make decisions based on a consensus government which is patiently waiting before taking action. Consensus does not compel unity after a decision has been made. Consensus waits for unity before making a decision.

Keep in mind this was not the flock of hundreds that met in Juniper's temple in Rome given by Constantine or followers focused on John Chrysostom, the Golden Tongued, in Constantinople, but a house church of perhaps twenty or thirty believers.

Consider the unity Paul is portraying to the divided Corinthians:

Since there is one bread, we who are many are one body; for we all partake of the one bread. I Corinthians 10:17.

For even as the body is one and yet has many members, and all the members of the body, though they are many, are one body, so also is Christ. For by one Spirit we were all baptized into one body, whether Jews or Greeks, whether slaves or free, and we were all made to drink of one Spirit. I Corinthians 12:12-13.

But God has so composed the body, giving more abundant honor to that member which lacked, so that there may be no division in the body, but that the members may have the same care for one another. I Corinthians 12:24-25.

Paul is making the point that the unity of the assembled believers is connected to their relationship with Christ. We distance ourselves from God upon our disunity. After all, by His nature He is One: the Father, Son and Holy Spirit. Therefore it seems evident government would necessarily come from a unified body. This is not governance by majority vote of a congregation but by consensus of everyone who is meeting together.

But if we wait for consensus we will never accomplish anything.

We need to trust Scripture in this teaching. In I Corinthians 11:2 Paul said, *...remember me in everything and hold firmly to the traditions, just as I delivered them to you.*

Perhaps God would have you wait at this time. God requires everything and yet so little. He desires our love, holiness in our lives, and asks us to witness to a lost world. If consensus is not obtained in these areas perhaps the elders have some shepherding to do. But most decisions churches make today should be tabled. Many church programs, new fellowship halls, fund raising and personnel changes will simply not be issues in Paul's model of church government and meetings.

The Corinthians focused on their teachers who were in the forefront. One would think this would facilitate consensus. Looking to leaders would bring unity to the Roman army, but looking to leaders did not work at Corinth. Perhaps they needed one leader over the other leaders. No, the branches needed to reconnect with the vine. Christ.

The Colossians followed religious authorities. This seems the perfect way to maintain unity and consensus if everyone in the church would submit. But instead Paul warned they were not holding to their Head (Christ) and were being defrauded of their prize in Colossians 2:18-19.

The question we have to answer in regards to governance is which is better. New Testament example and instruction or our innovative systems of church government?

Adding to God's Word

It is important that our understanding of Christ and our practice of following Him is based on the Bible and only the Bible. Attempts to <u>add</u> to what Scripture sufficiently teaches may lead us astray. A few verses that testify to the trustworthiness of His Word include:

...until heaven and earth pass away, not the smallest letter or stroke shall pass from the Law. Matthew 5:18. *Law* may refer to the first five books of the Bible or the entire Old Testament.

Heaven and earth will pass away, but My words will not pass away. Matthew 24:35.

...the scripture cannot be broken... John 10:35.

...all scripture is inspired by God... 2 Timothy 3:16-17.

These verses describe not only the reliability of the Old Testament but the reliability of the New Testament as we see in II Peter 3:16. There Peter wrote: *as they do the rest of the scriptures,* and he equated an apostle's epistles with the same sacred status as the Old Testament. As the Old Testament prophets, apostles were given God's Word in a supernatural sense which was affluently affirmed by the miracles they performed. II Corinthians 12:12.

Read Jesus explaining this inspiration to His apostles:

...it is not you who speak, but it is the Spirit of your Father which speaks in you. Matthew 10:19-20.

...I will give you utterance and wisdom which none of your opponents will be able to resist or refute. Luke 21:14-15.

Because these true apostles were identified from false apostles by the miracles they performed as well as their message, Christ's followers were able to identify which epistles were written with apostolic authority. Those tested epistles were later confirmed by church fathers as canon. But early church fathers did not determine canon! Church leaders only gave their assent to what had already been determined and accepted years earlier.

Of course, there was confusion concerning false and corrupted epistles just as there had been confusion concerning false apostles. But when church leaders confirmed canon in the fourth and fifth century they simply agreed with what small assemblies of believers have held since the first century. Before letters were sanctioned by church leaders at councils, such as the Synod of Hippo, these letters had already been evaluated by eye witnesses to the epistles' apostolic origins. We still have numerous records from the Synod of Carthage in 419 A.D. of Zahn saying:

'let this be sent to our brother and fellow-bishop, Boniface [of Rome], and to the other bishops of those parts, that they may confirm this Canon, for these are the things that we have received from our fathers to be read in church.'

Can you see from this quote that even though bishops at the Synod of Carthage confirmed our Canon, previous bodies of believers had already handed down those same books to be accepted as God's written Word?

We may not have the original Greek and Arabic documents but literally thousands of corroborating copied manuscripts testify to their existence. The consistency of copied Byzantine and even older Alexandrian manuscripts assure us that those original messages have been accurately preserved.

We trust that our Canon is perfect as it was written in those original autographs and see the consistency of corroborating Greek copies. But we do not trust in the perfection of men's translations. The fact that the original Greek manuscripts were perfect does not preclude a mistake from being made by bible translators.

Therefore it would be a mistake to not take into account the possibility of translation error where Greek words relating to the role of elders were inconsistently translated. An example is the translation of Greek word *proistemi* #4291b. We do not have an English cognate for this Greek word. The New Analytical Greek Lexicon by Wesley Perschbacher describes *proistemi* literally 'to set before' which has been interpreted with different definitions based on the context in both Scriptural and secular texts. One of those definitions is to preside, govern or superintend and the other is to undertake resolutely, to practice diligently or to maintain a practice. Translators determined which definition they would choose based on the context of each passage.

This Greek verb *proistemi* is used seven times in Scripture all by Paul. The same word is found in both Byzantine and Alexandrian texts (sometimes referred to as the received and critical text respectively). *Proistemi* was translated as 'rule' one time in the New American Standard and a few more times in the case of the New King James Version. Let's look at how New American Standard translations of *proistemi* varied and were contingent on the context.

For <u>believers</u> *proistemi* was translated as <u>engage</u>:

...those who believed God will be careful <u>to engage</u> (proistemi) in good deeds... Titus 3:8.

...our people must learn <u>to engage</u> (proistemi) in good deeds... Titus 3:14.

While for elders and deacons in a family context it was translated as manage:

...one who manages (proistemi) his own household... I Timothy 3:4.

...if a man does not know how to manage (proistemi) his own household... I Timothy 3:5.

...good managers (proistemi) of their children and households... I Timothy 3:12.

But for elders in a community of believers it was translated as rule:

The elders who rule (proistemi) well ...... I Timothy 5:17.

Do you see how Paul's word, proistemi, was subjectively translated based on the context in each case? But should not this Greek word be translated consistently unless there are overriding factors to the contrary? Especially in the same epistle written by the same author to the same readers!

The inconsistent translation of I Timothy 5:17 expands elders' duties from managing or maintaining to authoritatively ruling the body. It gives more sovereignty to elders than either of the other chosen translations (engage or manage) without New Testament corroboration and consequently contradicts Paul's warning against rulers in Colossians 2:8 ...See to it that no one takes *you captive…according to the elementary principles* (<u>rules</u>).

If *proistemi* conveys authoritative ruling in our assemblies, then that would legitimize *the places of honor* and *the chief seats in the synagogues* which Christ warned against in Matthew 23:5. But if the Pauline word 'to set before' consistently conveys practice, maintenance or management, then we have cohesion throughout the New Testament.

Augmenting *proistemi* to rule has the effect of circumventing Paul's directive to honor elders. The elders that Paul identifies to receive honor are different elders than those elders ruling with authority in our religious organizations today. Paul instructs us to honor older men in the faith, who in the final stage of their earthly life, work hard serving the body, leading (by example) and teaching the brethren. Our inconsistently translated text calls us to honor a ruler, a bishop or a magistrate.

The expansion of Paul's word from manage or maintain to rule is similar to the translation expansion in II Corinthians 11:8 where Paul's word for 'provisions' was translated as wages. There Paul is translated to say, *I robbed other churches by taking <u>wages</u> from them to serve you*. This translation clearly supports paying money to apostles. However the original Greek word 3800, *opsonion*, is actually 'cooked provisions' not wages.

Provisions are consistent with apostles being worthy of food and drink, which were called an apostle's wages in Luke 10:7. However monetary wages are not consistent with Christ's instruction to apostles in Matthew 10:9, *do not acquire gold, or silver, or copper for your money belts.* The slight expansion of the attributes of the original word to a paycheck suddenly casts doubt on the clear teaching of other New Testament passages such as I Peter 5:2 where Peter told elders: *shepherd the flock of God among you...voluntarily... and not for sordid gain.*

These inconsistent translations have the effect of expanding or adding to what Paul wrote. Our Father conveyed many times that we should never <u>add</u> to His Holy Word. It is sufficient as He gave it.

<u>*You shall not add to the word*</u> *which I am commanding you, nor take away from it, that you may keep the commandments of the Lord your God...* Deuteronomy 4.2.

Whatever I command you, you shall be careful to do; <u>*you shall not add to*</u> *nor take away from it.* Deuteronomy 12.32.

Every Word of God is tested...<u>*Do not add to His words*</u> *or He will reprove you, and you will be proved a liar.* Proverbs 30.5-6.

To everyone who hears the words of prophecy in this book: <u>if anyone adds to them,</u> God will add to him the plagues which are written in this book.... Revelation 22:18.

Read how adding to God's Word was part of the problem when brothers in Christ divisively turned to leaders in Corinth.

Now these things, brethren, I have figuratively applied to myself (Paul) *and Apollos for your sakes, so that in us you may <u>learn not to exceed what is written,</u> so that no one of you will become arrogant in behalf of one against another.* 1 Corinthians 4.6.

The Money

Well, if elders should not be the main teachers nor the authoritative rulers, then why were they paid?

Another characteristic of New Testament elders in contrast to today's counterpart is their lack of remuneration. They were not paid. As in II Thessalonians 3:7-9, they had been taught to follow Paul's example by not being a burden to anyone and by earning enough to give to those in need.

Today, church members give to preachers or elders. At Ephesus, elders gave to church members. Read Paul's conversation with the Ephesian elders about receiving money in Acts 20.

From Miletus he sent to Ephesus and called to him the elders of the church...20:17 ... I have coveted no one's silver or gold or clothes. 33. You yourselves know that these hands ministered to my own needs and to the men who were with me. 34. In everything I showed you that by working hard in this manner you must help the weak and remember the words of the Lord Jesus, that He Himself said, 'it is more blessed to give than receive.' 35.

Let's take another text. In I Corinthians 9:1-10 Paul proves his apostleship so that the Corinthians would follow his commands.

In verses 1-4 Paul says, ...*Am I not an apostle? ...My defense to those who examine me is this: Do we not have a right to eat and drink?*

In II Timothy 1:11 Paul told Timothy, ...*I was appointed a preacher and an apostle and a teacher...*

Paul is saying in I Corinthians 9 if he was a teacher or a preacher he would not have the right to food and drink. But as an apostle who had been sent personally by Christ and had the signs of a true apostle, II Corinthians 12:12, he deserved an apostle's wages. The fact that he deserved food and drink proved he was an apostle. But if he was only a teacher or preacher then, no, he would not deserve any food and drink.

Look at another text to make this clearer.

In I Peter 5:2 Peter is speaking specifically to elders and says, *shepherd the flock of God among you, exercising oversight not under compulsion, but voluntarily, according to the will of God; and not for sordid gain, but with eagerness.*

We all know what compulsion is and when we are paid to do something we better do it or return the money. The general meaning of the English word sordid is morally ignoble, base or vile. No paid Christian elder believes they minister for money but the fact remains that if they cash their paycheck they did it for money. I am not questioning their heart only their hermeneutics.

Galatians 6:6 has been used to support paying elders, *The one who is taught the word is to share all good things with the one who teaches him.*

But the Greek could just as easily read, "The one who is taught the word is to participate in good works with the one who teaches him." Go back and read the last few chapters if you don't have a concordance. Doesn't the text make more sense using the Greek general definitions? Even the previous verse, Galatians 6:5 insists, *each one will bear his own load.*

Here is a text most see as authorizing gain or profit for serving God as elders, I Timothy 5:17-18: *The elders who rule well are to be considered worthy of double honor, especially those who work hard at preaching and teaching. For the Scripture says, 'You shall not muzzle the ox while he is threshing', and 'the laborer is worthy of his wages.'*

In order to interpret these verses as advocating the receipt of money by preachers two texts seem to be overlooked. One, remember Paul is writing this to Timothy about the elders in Ephesus, I Timothy 1:3. These are the same Ephesian elders who were told not to receive but give in Acts 20:17.

Two, the receipt of money was precluded by Christ when he told the seventy, the apostles, *carry no money belt...* in Luke 10:4. This is even more explicit in Matthew 10:9, *do not acquire gold, or silver, or copper for your money belts.* So we can see that even though Christ stated, *for the laborer is worthy of his wages,* in Luke 10:7 to justify their board, He did not intend for them to collect money in exchange for God's word and that being the case then certainly Paul did not intend the honor shown in I Timothy 5:17-18 to be money.

This verse could command giving honor to hard working elders as honor was shown widows in I Timothy 5:3 by giving them food, or, as apostles were given food and drink in I Corinthians 9:4. But Paul did not intend this honor in 5:17 to be in the form of money, as in I Timothy 6:1, for surely honor due a master from a slave would not require money to the master. Children, likewise, do not honor their parents by paying their parents money.

If money was the intended honor in I Timothy 5:17 then we would have Scriptures which would contradict. These contradictions could not be resolved by saying undeserved wages were the wages paid when the gospel was distorted by an elder as some have voiced. Acts 20:29-35 and I Peter 5:2 preclude elder pay without mention of heresy. We are making a choice between the needy of this world and our favorite preachers or teachers, *where your treasure is, there your heart will be also* Matthew 6:21.

It may be helpful to understand apostles were given the right to eat, drink and have lodging by Jesus, *Stay in that house, eating and drinking what they give you; for the laborer is worthy of his wages.* Luke 10:7. This is the basis of Paul's argument in I Corinthians 9.

But there were also false apostles hoping for gain. *Such men are false apostles, deceitful workers, disguising themselves as apostles of Christ.* II Corinthians 11:13.

Paul had to address this by qualifying who was an apostle, *The signs of a true apostle were performed among you with all perseverance, by signs and wonders and miracles.* II Corinthians 12:12.

Because false apostles could enjoy authority, free food or some other gain, it was an easy next step to ask for money because the <u>Didache,</u> which is not inspired but one of our oldest Christian documents, in section 11:5-9 includes this instruction:

> 'Let every apostle, when he cometh to you, be received as the Lord; but he shall not abide more than a single day, or if there be need, another, but if he abide three days, he is a false prophet. And when he departeth let the apostle receive nothing save bread until he findeth shelter; but <u>if he ask money, he is a false apostle.</u>'

If an apostle should not receive money in a very developed Roman world that utilized currency over a barter system in return for information on eternal life, then it would appear obvious neither should an elder, regardless how we enjoy his example or preaching.

This lack of financial payment to teachers, preachers and elders corroborates the evidence that they were simply a part of the body. There was no difference in importance or prominence of the teaching gift in the assembly over any other gifts. Yes, we should honor elders and teachers, but not allow favoritism over other believers during the assembly, regardless of how small we consider their gifts. All are simply branches holding to the vine.

The role Paul prescribed for elders and teachers was no more prominent than the role of other members of the body, and this lack of monetary remuneration supports this conclusion. If we reconsidered this issue, our witness to a cynical world would change overnight. Consider if eighty percent of church contributions are consumed by buildings and church staff how we could affect the world if those numbers were reversed by believers assembling in small unpaid groups.

If your Individual Retirement Account had administrative costs of eighty percent each year, you would reconsider your choice of IRA administrator. Please reconsider the investment in your relationship with Christ.

A Warning

In the Book of Revelation the triumphant Christ
has encouragement for the Ephesian church and a
stern warning for the church in Pergamum for their
different responses to the deeds and teaching of the
Nicolaitans.

To the Church in Ephesus Jesus says:

*Yet this you do have, that you hate the deeds of the
<u>Nicolaitans,</u> which I also hate.* Revelation 2:6.

To the Church in Pergamum He has this to say:

*...you also have some who in the same way hold the
teaching of the <u>Nicolaitans</u>. Therefore repent; or else I
am coming to you quickly, and I will make war against
them with the sword of My mouth.* Revelation 2:15-
16.

Who were these Nicolaitans and why did Jesus
hate their deeds and warn the Pergamum church
about their teaching? Commentators debate the
answer and often suggest possible identities of the
Nicolaitans while describing these Johannine
passages as surprisingly mysterious.

Certainly care should be taken when interpreting
two thousand year old texts for which limited
biblical references are available as corroboration in
order that Scripture might interpret Scripture. But

what if these passages recorded by the beloved Apostle John were given not to be mysterious but rather plain and clear?

If this were the case, then let's look at the simple meaning of the word Nicolaitan. This will give insight into why our Lord hates their deeds. The original Greek word *nicolaitan* is composed of two words, *nikao*, Greek word #3528, meaning conquer or subdue and *laiton* #2992 meaning people. We get our English term laity from the latter.

Whether Jesus was referring to the role of a certain group of believers or whether He was using the name of an individual the effect is the same. The choice by Jesus of using *nicolaitan*, as conquerors of laity, or as an individual's name would be consistent with other passages inspired by His Spirit. He often used a descriptive name in the Bible to portray the essence of a person to us. Consider that Luke wrote to Theophilus in the Gospel of Luke and also in Acts of the Apostles. *Theophilus* in the Greek means friend of God or lover of God. The plain meaning of this word emphasizes the personal application of those books to each believer.

In the same way if we use the plain meaning of *nicolaitan*, conquerors of laity, how then are the laity conquered or subdued within the context of a Christian Church? The laity could be conquered by convincing the bride of Christ that she should look to teachers or overseers in order to please the Bridegroom.

It would be an error to attribute such a conquering to clergy alone because the passages do not indicate this. As at Colossae both clergy and laity are involved in the process of dividing a local body into two tiers. This indicates a *quid pro quo* is taking place. While some desire to lead the flock in spiritual duties, there are also those who desire to depend on teachers as at Corinth and Colossae or to hand over their spiritual duties to professionals.

Having a leader take responsibility for our duties does not discharge our obligation. We are not relieved of our individual duties of participating in the corporate meeting when we pay someone to teach, preach or sing.

...when you assemble, each one has a psalm, has a teaching, has a revelation, has a tongue, has an interpretation...for edification... I Corinthians 14:26.

...if all prophesy, and an unbeliever or an ungifted man enters, he is convicted by all... I Corinthians 14:24.

The hope of glory you have is *Christ in you.* Colossians 1:27. What does this indwelling say about the position we hold in relation to one another as we assemble together?

What does this indwelling say about the one-on-one relationship with Christ that He designed and purposes? Our God is a jealous God and He says of His bride, *My sheep hear My voice ...and they follow Me.* John 10:27. Not a teacher or leader.

Would we appreciate another man stepping forward to explain the application of our love letters to our fiancée. Or would we be pleased if our betrothed depended on another in her response to our letters? Yes, teaching one another is crucial. Yes, the Ethiopian eunuch appropriately asked for explanation and received it in Acts 8. But after the Ethiopian believed in Christ, the Spirit carried his teacher, Phillip, away leaving the new believer in the good hands of His Holy Spirit and His written Word.

Whether conquerors of laity utilize teaching to draw disciples to themselves as at Corinth or a governing authority as at Colossae, a nicolaitan leader is a hindrance to the bride's one-on-one relationship with Christ. Although used by God in the Old Testament, a priestly caste wedged between the bride and groom is not the model we see in the New Covenant.

The Apostle Paul commanded participation of everyone in the assembly which allowed an orderly opportunity for us to confess the name of Jesus and thereby please Him by loving and encouraging one another. But Paul did not preclude teaching and shepherding. The use of a clergy class simply goes too far by assuming the laity is too busy or spiritually incompetent to teach one another.

The use of a clergy class may also presume some gifts, perhaps the teaching gift, are the more important gifts, thereby, uniquely qualifying the holders as decision or policy makers for the entire flock. Instead of a body of believers lifting up Scripture together to determine doctrine and practice, a clergy class might rule on these issues instead.

If we interpret these Johannine verses using their plain Greek meaning, we might find ourselves considering what characteristics a church would have if they tolerated *nicolaitan* deeds or teaching. Certainly characteristics could include reservations of activities for clergy which were intended to be practiced by every individual believer.

For instance we might see 1) the limitation of who could teach or speak in the assembly; 2) the limitation of who could administer the Lord's Supper or the limitation of when believers could observe communion; 3) the limitation of who could perform baptisms; 4) the limitation of which nonessential doctrines that believers could hold while still maintaining full fellowship with other church members or while maintaining all of the rights of church membership; 5) the limitation of who would be recipients of charity; or we might see 6) the diversion of money from biblical charity to conquerors of the laity.

Yes, this conquering of laity might involve some believers (laity) giving money to other believers (a clergy caste). You can see in Revelation 2:14, 15, that Nicolaitans were linked to Balaam who in the book of Numbers received money in exchange for his blessing and prophecy: ...*who hold the teaching of* _Balaam_...*you also have some who in the* _same_ _way_ *hold the teaching of the* _Nicolaitans_....

This characteristic of Balaam is also a concern in II Peter 2:15 ...*the way of Balaam, the son of Beor, who loved the wages of unrighteousness*...

Consider again Pauline instruction specifically to the Ephesian elders in Acts chapter 20. The Ephesian elders had been warned for three years that some would rise from within the church with an interest in receiving, not giving. Acts 20:30-31, 34-35. Paul prophesied that these would seek to draw away disciples to themselves. It appears the Ephesian church fought against this practice which pleased our Lord because years later John reports that Jesus commends that same church in Ephesus:

Yet this you do have, that you hate the deeds of the _Nicolaitans,_ *which I also hate.* Revelation 2:6.

Complete in Christ

If we take isolated Scriptures without comparing all New Testament passages, we may arrive at the conclusion that the elder is the primary means God uses to build our relationship with Christ.

He gave some as apostles, and some as prophets, and some as evangelists, and some as pastors and teachers, for the equipping of the saints for the work of service, to the building up of the body of Christ; until we all attain to the unity of the faith and the knowledge of the Son of God, to a mature man, to the measure of the stature which belongs to the fullness of Christ. Ephesians 4:11-13.

While God no doubt uses men in our lives for His glory it is crucial we keep in mind who is our Bread of Life and Teacher. We have a direct relationship with our Creator with no mediator except Christ Himself. One of the great mysteries of Scripture, similar to Christ being both God and man or God's sovereignty in salvation while holding man responsible, is the edification of God's people in light of their completeness in Christ.

Certainly just as the body must not take their eyes off Christ even for an Apollos, so we must not forget that the hapless, uneducated basket case of a believer in our assembly (for such were many of us) is a child of the king and is complete in Christ while we attempt to love, shepherd and even be edified by that brother.

This juxtaposition appears in Colossians. While Paul prayed and taught to present the believer as bearing fruit and increasing in knowledge he also recognized the completeness we have in Christ now.

Notice our responsibility in this verse:

We proclaim Him, admonishing every man and teaching every man with all wisdom, so that we may present every man complete in Christ. Colossians 1:28.

See God's completed work in the believer:

In Him you have been made complete, and He is the head over all rule and authority. Colossians 2:10.

We should never underestimate the Spirit's work when He revealed to us the character of Christ. If we do, the Apostle John offers proofs for us to know whether our salvation is true by looking at evidence of this completeness in I John. I John 5:13.

As elders if we don't recognize a disciple's completeness in Christ we may gravitate toward an improper role of Mr. holy spirit, Jr. in our shepherding duties. Through regimen or oversight we, like the Colossians, may coerce the believer to conform outwardly but that is not the goal. The Pharisees outwardly were very godly but inwardly they did not please our Father. Although we rebuke, exhort and hold each other accountable, this is to hold one another accountable to what we already desire.

Completeness, which is the indwelling of the Spirit, is a different concept than justification, which was accomplished upon Christ's crucifixion and resurrection. Neither is completeness the same as sanctification, which is considered a progressive process over time by some but which others interpret as a setting apart.

Look at Scriptures which describe this completeness. I will try to not include verses that are addressing our positional standing before God, often referred to as justification, but some verses may indicate both concepts of justification and completeness.

For of His fullness we have all received, and grace upon grace. John 1:16.

Let us therefore, as many as are perfect, (complete) *have this attitude...* Philippians 3:15.

Seeing that His divine power has granted to us everything pertaining to life and godliness... II Peter 1:3.

And concerning you, my brethren, I myself also am convinced that you yourselves are full of goodness, filled with all knowledge and able also to admonish one another. Romans 15:14.

So then let no one boast in men. For <u>all things belong to you</u>, whether Paul or Apollos or Cephas or the world or life or death or things present or things to come; <u>all things belong to you</u>, and you belong to Christ; and Christ belongs to God. I Corinthians 3:21-23.

As elders, how dare we put ourselves in a position of authority over other believers who are complete with Christ's indwelling? As believers why would we turn after experiencing the teaching of the Holy Spirit to any man no matter how *eloquent and mighty* his preaching?

To further understand the New Testament role of elder, in contrast to the Old Testament Levitical priesthood, let's remember that since Pentecost the believer has God's Law written in his heart.

I am not speaking of God's law in the general sense as it was given to all mankind as shown in Romans 2:14-15, *when gentiles who do not have the Law do instinctively the things of the Law, these, not having the Law, are a law to themselves, in that they show the work of the Law written in their hearts, their conscience bearing witness and their thoughts alternately accusing or else defending them.*

I am speaking of God's law in the specific sense of his regenerate children who have the Holy Spirit dwelling in them, prophecy of which we see fulfilled in Hebrews 10:16, *This is the covenant that I will make with them after those days, says the Lord; I will put my Laws upon their heart, and on their mind I will write them.*

Consider these passages:

...The Holy Spirit, whom the Father will send in My name, He will teach you all things... John 14:26.

But when He, the Spirit of Truth, comes, He will guide you into all the truth... John 16:13.

Now we have received, not the spirit of the world, but the Spirit who is from God, so that we may know the things freely given to us by God...not in words taught by human wisdom... I Corinthians 2:12-13.

Now as to the love of the brethren, you have no need for anyone to write to you, for you yourselves are taught by God to love one another. I Thessalonians 4:9.

...if in anything you have a different attitude, God will reveal that also to you... Philippians 3:15.

As for you, the anointing which you received from Him abides in you, and you have no need for anyone to teach you; but as His anointing teaches you about all things, and is true and is not a lie, and just as it has taught you, you abide in Him. I John 2:27.

...after those days, says the LORD: I will put My laws into their minds, and I will write them on their hearts...

And they shall not teach everyone his fellow citizen, and everyone his brother... Hebrews 8:10-11.

Consider what I say, for the lord will give you understanding in everything. Remember Jesus Christ... II Timothy 2:7-8.

Even though our Father may have given an elder the privilege of being used in the edification of many believers, those same believers would have been equally edified if they had been alone on a Pacific Island without a leader, pastor or mentor teaching or directing them. This is God's promise.

Of course this is not to say we, as believers, do not grow in conformity to Christ. Peter encouraged holiness in the believer, I Peter 1:14-16, and yet Peter seemed more concerned the believer might forget than he was concerned the believer should learn something new.

For he who lacks these qualities is blind or short-sighted, having forgotten his purification from his former sins. II Peter 1:9.

When the Corinthians were following men and being divisive, Paul reminded them, *Do you not know that you are a temple of God and that the Spirit of God dwells in you?* I Corinthians 3:16.

When the Colossians were following men and being defrauded of their prize Paul reminded them, *If you have been raised up with Christ, keep seeking the things above.* Colossians 3:1.

Should We Follow
Paul's Model for Elders?

Are the Scripture passages we have discussed depicting consensual, interactive assemblies and the responsibilities of every believer <u>prescriptive</u> for us to follow or simply <u>descriptive</u> of a time and place far away? Are they a mandate to be obeyed or are we reading too much into the passages? Ultimately each one of us must decide but Paul's warning from I Corinthians and Colossians is that our relationship with Christ is at stake.

I submit that in the very context of warning the Corinthians about following leaders Paul calls them to follow his example exalting Christ and encouraging one another as unpaid, unpolished participators in the assembly.

Therefore I exhort you, be imitators of me. I Corinthians 4:16.

This is not an isolated teaching from Paul. On numerous occasions with apostolic authority he commanded us to follow his example as well as the model he gave for assembling as Christ's body.

Be imitators of me, just as I also am of Christ. I Corinthians 11:1

...hold firmly to the traditions, just as I delivered them to you. I Corinthians 11:2

But if one is inclined to be contentious, we have no other practice, nor have the churches of God. I Corinthians 11:16

Brethren, join in following my example, and observe those who walk according to the pattern you have in us... Philippians 3:17

The things you have learned and received and heard and seen in me, practice these things. Philippians 4:9.

...hold to the traditions which you were taught, whether by word of mouth or by letter from us. II Thessalonians 2:15.

you yourselves know how you ought to follow our example... II Thessalonians 3:7.

nor did we eat anyone's bread without paying for it, but with labor and hardship we kept working night and day so that we would not be a burden to any of you; not because we do not have the right to this, but in order to offer ourselves as a model for you, so that you would follow our example. II Thessalonians 3:8, 9.

There is no reason for us to be hesitant or timid in following Paul's teaching except a lack of faith in our Father's trustworthiness. It is clear that Paul taught with Christ's Spirit and we know that our Savior has our best in store. Even though I am lacking necessary persuasive words, I confidently end with Christ's own appeal knowing that His Word and Spirit are effectual to those that love Him.

Come to Me, all who are weary and heavy-laden, for I am gentle and humble in heart, and you will find rest for your souls. For My yoke is easy and My burden is light. Matthew 11:28-30.

Jesus made His appeal in the context of praising our Father for hiding His character and purpose from the wise and intelligent in Matthew 11:25. Should we be relying on the wise and intelligent to rule and teach us when the Word and His fellowship are waiting?

Matthew 25:21 reminds us of the reward for following Christ. *Well done, good and faithful slave. You were faithful with a few things...enter into the joy of your master.* Whether we call ourselves leaders or followers what is the danger of not following apostolic teaching on the role of elders?

The danger of not glorifying and enjoying Christ.

The Corinthian believers were avid in their theology. They were seeking solid food. Yet Paul spent four chapters of Holy Writ warning them not to lift up very godly men. In comparison he only portioned one small chapter, chapter five, to the lack of church discipline in the case of a believer's boasted incest.

Paul struggled in his fear that those in Colossae were following teachers and authorities and thereby were being defrauded of the prize in Colossians 2:18.

Have you listened to sermons, compared teachings, become very discerning, but wonder if there is more of Christ and body life to enjoy? Have you been faithful for scheduled meetings, contributed to church programs, followed regimen for memorization of Scripture and catechism, but do not enjoy a deep relationship with many members of your church? Perhaps you, like many of us, are a Corinthian or Colossian and we need to get back to Christ.

The Corinthians were distracted from Christ toward teachers and the Colossians turned from Christ to ecclesiastical authorities after Peter, Paul and Apollos had pointed them to our Savior. Therefore we should not be so naïve to think that after repositioning the role of elders to follow Paul's commands that assemblies would not have problems.

But what if…

Appendix A
Appointment of Elders

Why would elders have been 'appointed' if they were not primarily teachers or if they were not to hold an ecclesiastical office? Titus 1:5 *For this reason I left you in Crete, that you would set in order what remains and __appoint__ elders in every city as I directed you.*

Although Greek word #2525, *kathistemi*, is used in some manuscripts the Greek word translated 'appoint' in Titus 1:5 in <u>Interlinear NIV Parallel New Testament</u> and <u>Greek to English Interlinear of the New King James Version New Testament</u> is Greek word #2688 *katastema* with the general meaning of demeanor, not appoint. It can also mean the state, condition or mien. By translating the text according to the Greek general meanings we read, *For this reason I left you in Crete, in order that you __determine the condition__ of the elders and put in order anything lacking.*

This definition is obtained by locating the Greek word in the interlinear translations and reading the general meanings in <u>New Analytical Greek Lexicon.</u>

The other instance of the word appointment in the New Testament is in Acts 14:23 when another Greek word, #5500, *cheirotoneo*, may be translated as 'laying on of hands' or 'extending of hands,' as in a vote, but does not imply an ecclesiastical office.

When they had appointed (layed hands on) *elders for them in every church, having prayed with fasting, they commended them to the Lord...*

Appendix B
Other Scripture Passages that Speak to the Issue of Gain by Elders

Christ told us how to use money without mention of church staffs and buildings. It is not that we should never spend resources on these, but our first priority is to follow His teaching. As we seek a relationship with Him we should not spend on what we think best before spending on what He said and in the way He said. By giving in the manner He commanded we will show our trust in Him.

Perhaps these verses will be helpful as you consider New Testament teaching on giving to elders.

...as you go, preach,... freely you received, freely give. Matthew 10:7-8.

He who is a hired hand, and not a shepherd, who is not the owner of the sheep, sees the wolf coming, and leaves the sheep and flees, and the wolf snatches them and scatters them. He flees because he is a hired hand and is not concerned about the sheep. John 10:12-13.

...just as I also please all men in all things, not seeking my own profit but the profit of the many. I Corinthians 10:33.

...for we are not like many, peddling the word of God. II Corinthians 2:17.

...I will not be a burden to you for I do not seek what is yours, but you; for children are not responsible to save up for their parents, but parents for their children. I will most gladly spend and be expended for your souls. If I love you more, am I to be loved less? ... Certainly I have not taken advantage of you through any of those whom I have sent to you, have I? I urged Titus to go, and I sent the brother with him. Titus did not take any advantage of you, did he? II Corinthians 12:14-18.

...for we never came with flattering speech, as you know, nor with a pretext for greed, God is witness....even though as apostles of Christ we might have asserted our authority....For you recall, brethren, our labor and hardship, how working night and day so as not to be a burden to any of you, we proclaimed to you the gospel of God. I Thessalonians 2:5-9.

...make it your ambition to lead a quiet life and attend to your own business and work with your hands, just as we commanded you, so that you will behave properly toward outsiders and not be in any need. I Thessalonians 4:11-12.

In II Thessalonians 3:6-15 Paul told the Thessalonians to remember how he preached, taught, shepherded and worked to pay his own way. He then told them to follow his example. If anyone did not follow his example then they were to be admonished as a brother.

...who suppose that godliness is a means of gain but godliness actually is a means of great gain when accompanied by contentment. I Timothy 6:5-6.

...the overseer must be above reproach as God's steward, not self-willed, not quick-tempered, not addicted to wine, not pugnacious, not fond of sordid (vile) *gain.* Titus 1:7.

...who must be silenced because they are upsetting whole families, teaching things they should not teach for the sake of sordid (vile) *gain.* Titus 1:11.

...and in their greed they will exploit you with false words... II Peter 2:3.

...having a heart trained in greed... II Peter 2:14.

...the way of Balaam, the son of Beor, who loved the wages of unrighteousness... II Peter 2:15.

...these are springs without water... II Peter 2:17.

...for pay they have rushed headlong into the error of Balaam... Jude 11.

...clouds without water...autumn trees without fruit... Jude 12.

Appendix C
Scriptural Examples of Missionary Support

Diligently help Zenas the lawyer and Apollos on their way so that nothing is lacking for them. Our people must also learn to engage in good deeds to meet pressing needs, so that they will not be unfruitful. Titus 3:13-14.

...you will do well to send them on their way in a manner worthy of God. For they went out for the sake of the Name, accepting nothing from the Gentiles. Therefore we ought to support such men... III John 6b-8.

Appendix D
Greek Word *hegeomai* Translated as Leader

In Hebrews 13 a plural form of Greek word *#2233*, *hegeomai*, is written in three different cases (accusative, dative, and genitive). It is important that the role we envision for non-Christian leaders does not cause us to misinterpret and thereby apply *hegeomai* in a manner which contradicts the totality of New Testament teaching regarding Christian elders or leaders.

...remember those who led you ... Hebrews 13:7.
...obey your leaders... Hebrews 13:17.
...greet your leaders ... Hebrews 13:24.

We have already discussed the Greek word for obey in Hebrews 13:17 and shown that this word should actually be translated as trust and should not be interpreted as a military command to obey unlike the Greek word, for instance, used when children are instructed to obey in Ephesians 6:1. This is important because scholars often and appropriately translate a passage contingent on the context presupposing how we should respond to an elder.

If we choose to use the definition of *hegeomai* to understand the role of elders or leaders, then we have two choices.

First as chronologically leading:

Hegeomai is defined as to lead, go before, go first, or lead the way. The first question is whether this leading, going before, being first or leading the way should be interpreted appositionally, as in leading from a podium, or chronologically.

Used in a chronological sense Paul or the writer of Hebrews would be speaking of those who have known Christ a longer time than more recent converts. This definition is encouraged by the text itself in Hebrews 13:7, *remember those who led you, who spoke the word of God to you; and considering the result of their conduct, imitate their faith.* We can see from this verse that those who led had gone before the readers chronologically because the text reads, *...led, ...remember those, ...spoke, ...the result of their conduct...,* all indicating past tense actions. This definition would also be synonymous with the Greek word definition of an elder as an older man or the contextual definition of an elder as a man older in the faith.

Second as leading from a positional or presiding role:

The definition of *hegeomai* to lead, go before, go first, or lead the way could be translated as a positional or presiding role. It is important that if we choose to base our understanding of an elder's role upon this Greek word definition of *hegeomai*, then the role should not be understood in a manner which would contradict Paul's instruction to the Corinthians or Colossians. In other words, leadership as such should encourage assembly participation as well as consensus governance. Thus the duty of elders should include discouraging traditional leadership roles of a dominate teacher or a governing position in the assembly.

In addition to using a lexicon's definition to determine the role of *hegeomai*, we could also utilize the interpretation principle of allowing Scripture to interpret Scripture. In this case we would have three available passages for insight.

And you, Bethlehem, Land of Judah, are by no means least among the leaders (hegeomai) of Judah; for out of you shall come forth a Ruler... Mathew 2:6.

...And they began calling Barnabas, Zeus, and Paul, Hermes, because he was the chief (hegeomai) speaker. Acts 14:12.

...and he made him (Joseph) *governor (hegeomai) over Egypt and all his household.* Acts 7:10.

In the case of Joseph's role in Acts 7:10 we should not be influenced in any direction by the translation of *epi* as over. *Epi* is used nearly 200 times in the New Testament (often as on, in or of) and was translated as the preposition over in only five cases. Also the fact that Joseph's household was in the same position as Joseph in or over Egypt brings more questions as to the exact role being referenced in this verse.

However a higher hermeneutic principle than using Greek word definitions or allowing Scripture to interpret Scripture is to simply follow the clear instruction of Christ. Consider how our Creator defines *hegeomai* in Luke 22:25, 26:

And He said to them, "The kings of the Gentiles lord it over them; and those who have authority over them are called 'Benefactors.' But it is not this way with you, but the one who is the greatest among you must become like the youngest, and the leader (<u>hegeomai</u>) like the servant. For who is greater, the one who reclines at the table or the one who serves? Is it not the one who reclines at the table? But I am among you as the one who serves."

Younger children offer assistance, encouragement and even gentle rebukes but they do not presume to teach over nor exercise authority over adults in their family. We have a choice as to how we apply *hegeomai* in non-Christian roles. But for Christian leadership roles in the assembly of believers who are following Christ and His Word we really do not have a choice. Thanks to all of you who serve us and Him in this manner.

Recommended Sites

CMA Resources
www.cmaresources.org

House 2 House Online Magazine
www.house2house.tv

House Church
www.housechurch.com

House-Church
www.house-church.org

House Church Canada
www.housechurch.ca

New Testament Reformation Fellowship
www.ntrf.org

Present Testimony Ministry
www.ptmin.org

Searching Together
www.searchingtogether.org

Simple Church
www.simplechurch.com

Author Bio

The author submitted his life to Christ at the age of 27 while reading alone in a childhood Bible. Subsequently losing his job he then worked as a lumberjack for eight years. In 1991 he passed the Certified Public Accountant exam and is now a partner in an accounting firm in Brandon, Mississippi.

Married with four daughters and one son-in-law he has served as a ruling elder in the Presbyterian Church of America and as an elder in a Reformed Baptist Church. Since 2005 he has home churched with families in the Jackson, Mississippi area.

Made in the USA
Lexington, KY
29 March 2014